SAINTLY TALES

AND

LEGENDS

To Davina L.R.
For Daisy, Isabelle and Archie
Carter C.B.

Library of Congress Cataloging-in-Publication Data

Rock, Lois, 1953-
 Saintly tales and legends / Lois Rock ; illustrated by Christina Balit.— 1st North American ed.
  p. cm.
 ISBN 0-8198-7083-8
 1. Christian saints—Legends. I. Balit, Christina. II. Title.
 BX4658.R63 2004
 282'.092'2—dc22

                          2004006649

ISBN 0-8198-7083-8

Original edition published in English under the title *Lion Book of Tales and Legends* by Lion Publishing plc, Oxford, England

First North American edition, 2004

Text copyright © 2003 Lois Rock

Illustration copyright © 2003 Christina Balit

Copyright © Lion Publishing plc 2004

The moral rights of the author and illustrator have been asserted.

"P" and PAULINE are registered trademarks of the Daughters of St. Paul

Published by Pauline Books & Media, 50 Saint Pauls Avenue, Boston, MA 02130-3491

Printed and bound in India

www.pauline.org

Pauline Books & Media is the publishing house of the Daughters of St. Paul, an international congregation of women religious serving the Church with the communications media.

1 2 3 4 5 6 7 8 9   11 10 09 08 07 06 05 04

SAINTLY TALES

AND

LEGENDS

Lois Rock
Illustrated by Christina Balit

Pauline
BOOKS & MEDIA
Boston

Contents

The Cinderella Saint

The Legend of Saint Germaine

THE LITTLE GIRL sat out on the hillside watching her sheep. Nuzzling by her side was an orphan lamb.

"It's hard being an orphan, isn't it?" said the girl, whose name was Germaine. "My mother died when I was only tiny, and my stepmother doesn't like me at all."

She sighed. "I hope I'm being a good stepmother to you, little lamb."

The creature bleated happily, and Germaine smiled.

Into the quiet of the countryside came the sound of a bell. "Oh, it's time for me to go to church," she said to the lamb. "But don't worry. I won't be long, and my guardian angel will take care of you and all the sheep till I return."

She jumped up and planted her crook in the ground before running down the hill. The sheep grazed in safety until Germaine returned to lead them on to fresh pasture. Later, as the sun began to sink, Germaine drove the flock back down to the fold close to her father's house.

"Hurry up, you lazy girl!" Germaine's stepmother said angrily. "Get on and make supper for us."

The stepmother hated Germaine, and she slapped her out of spite as she passed.

Germaine shrugged and set about stirring up the fire before chopping vegetables for a savoury stew. Then she lifted the plate off the bowl where she had left the bread dough to rise since the morning and began to shape the loaves.

"How long are we going to have to wait?" snarled her stepmother.

"Supper will be ready by the time Father returns," Germaine assured her.

Her stepmother scowled and returned to nursing her baby. Germaine prepared the meal and cleaned the kitchen while it cooked. She laid the table for her father and her stepmother and her stepmother's children. When she saw her father returning, she hurried to have everything ready just as he entered the house.

"I don't like this," whined one of the children, as they began to eat.

"Germaine, this stew is awful," scolded her stepmother.

"Seems good to me," said Germaine's father, idly shaking salt onto his serving.

"Don't take her side," hissed his wife. "She never seasons it right."

"I would be able to make it better if I could taste it before I served you," explained Germaine.

"DON'T BE SO INSOLENT!" shouted her stepmother. "You'd eat all the best bits. You serve us, and then you can have anything left over. Now get on with the other things that need doing."

Germaine set to feeding the dogs that had returned with her father and rushed outside to scurry the chickens into the henhouse before locking them in safely for the night.

"Don't think you can leave us with this mess," shouted her stepmother from the door, but already Germaine was running to gather the dishes.

As the household went to bed, Germaine reached for the blanket she kept in a high cupboard and prepared to sleep in the little alcove below the stairs.

"Get out," called her stepmother from upstairs. "The dogs will need to sleep there. Get out and go to the stable. It's warm enough."

Germaine scuttled away. She could never do anything right as far as her stepmother was concerned, but the stable was cosy and it was more peaceful.

She smiled up at the stars as she ran across the yard to find shelter. "God and the angels are in heaven watching over me," she told herself happily as she snuggled down in the straw.

Every day it was the same. Germaine rose early to rouse the fire and start the porridge and the bread for the day. Then she went out to milk the cows and let the chickens out to forage. If she was lucky, she might find some stale crusts and bits of cheese that the children had left from the day before to be her food for the day. Then she would set off to look after her sheep, pausing only to go to church when the bell rang for daily Mass.

Often, beggars would gather at the church door, hoping to receive gifts. Germaine was happy to share her food with any who were hungry. "I only wish the food were nicer," she apologized.

Years went by, and Germaine grew from a girl to a young woman. Her stepmother grew crabbier and ever more jealous. One winter's morning, when the world was brown and grey and edged with frost, she watched as Germaine darted around the farmyard, busy with her morning jobs before setting off with her sheep. She noticed that Germaine had gathered up her apron in front of her to hold something.

"Thief!" she cried. "What are you trying to steal? Are you taking more of our bread for your filthy beggars?"

She strode out and roughly pulled Germaine's arm so the apron spilled out what was within. Out tumbled a cascade of spring flowers.

The older woman gasped. "Where did you find these?" she asked, trembling. In the barren landscape, there were none to be seen.

Germaine smiled. "They are a gift to me from God and his angels," she replied.

Her stepmother faltered, for as Germaine spoke her face seemed to shine with a special light.

That evening, still shaking from what she had seen, she invited Germaine into the house.

"I've made up a bed for you," she mumbled.

"Oh, I won't be needing it," said Germaine. "If I am to stay indoors, the place below the stairs is comfortable enough."

She lay down to sleep, smiling at the unaccustomed warmth of her surroundings.

In the night, an angel came. "Germaine," said the angel, "we have made for you in heaven a bed softer than a cloud. Come. You have worked long enough in this world."

So Germaine was taken to heaven, and at the place where her body was buried on earth, people came from far and near to seek God's blessing.

Abelard and the Three Gifts

A Folk Tale

WHEN ABELARD WAS young, he lived in a little house with his mother and his father. They provided him with everything he needed.

When he was still just a boy, both his parents died, and Abelard was left an orphan.

However, he was not entirely alone for, at his christening, his mother and father had chosen for him three godparents who lived in a neighboring country. When these three heard the sad news, they each came in turn to offer what help they could.

The first one arrived with tears in her eyes. "What a tragedy," she wept. "I have come to take care of you till you are older. Look, I have brought you a quilt that is soft and deep. You can wrap yourself in its cosy warmth and protect yourself from the cruel bitter world."

Abelard took the quilt gladly. The dark days of mourning were eased a little by the soft comfort of the quilt, and his godmother did all she could to protect him from any more sorrow and harm.

When Abelard was almost grown up, the second of his godparents came to visit. His godfather came striding up the path to the house, calling out his greeting, and knocked firmly on the door.

"Come, Abelard," he said. "We all have to make our way in the world some time. You are young and strong, and I can help you find work on the farms and in the workshops. In time you will have to choose a trade for yourself and earn your own living."

Then his godfather opened the pack he was carrying and brought out a pair of stout leather boots. "Here," he said. "You will need these as a working man."

The boots fitted well, and Abelard did as his godfather instructed him.

He learned how to care for the sheep on the hills and how to steer the plough through the fields in the valley. He learned how to sow seed and reap the harvest.

He learned how to fell trees and saw them into planks and fashion the wood into the everyday things that people needed.

He learned how to set the sails of the windmill to grind the corn to make flour.

After three years, he said to his godfather, "I am a grown man now, and you have helped me to learn so many things. I am ready to go to work for my fortune in a new land."

His godfather readily agreed, and together they made the necessary preparations.

At last, Abelard was ready to set off for the port from which he would sail. He packed his quilt, and was cheered to remember the love he had received as a child.

He laced his boots and felt a wave of confidence that he had within him the ability to succeed in whatever the future might hold.

But as he left the little valley behind, he felt lost. Where was he going? What would the future hold?

It was then that the third of his godparents arrived to walk with him a little way.

This godparent was an old man, grey-haired and wrinkled, and slightly stooping. Yet Abelard saw at once that he had eyes of the clearest blue, which danced and twinkled, and the gentle and wise smile of one who knows and understands all things.

"You are about to begin a great journey into this world," he explained to Abelard, "and it will not be long before I shall make my journey into the next. But before we part, accept my gift."

He pulled from his pocket a simple wooden flute and played a merry melody. "Keep this with you always and learn to play your own tunes," he explained. "Sometimes your heart will be heavy and sometimes your body will be weary, but this music will always help your spirit to dance."

So with these three gifts, Abelard sailed away.

The Giant by the River

A Legend of Saint Christopher

LONG AGO, in a country to the east, there lived a giant. His appearance was so frightening that no one wanted him to live close to them. Mocked and scorned, he made his home high among the mountains.

While he was hiding in his lair, his heart grew hard and cold. One night, in a dream, the Devil came to him.

"You must be lonely," said the Devil soothingly. "But I will be a friend to you. Serve me, and you will have all you need."

"How will that happen?" asked the giant gruffly.

"Look," said the Devil. "Many travellers come along this mountain road—pilgrims and merchants, soldiers and messengers. You are strong and bold: you can ambush them and rob them… and so pay back the cruelty you have been shown."

So the next day, when he awoke, the giant went and hid beside the road. Soon a wealthy merchant came riding by. The giant stepped out and lifted the man off his horse. He held him upside down till the gold ran out of his pockets. Then he flung the man down the hillside and set his horse off at a gallop.

The giant laughed as he strode back to his lair. From now on he would be rich and he would have his revenge on the world of people who hated him.

So he became a bandit, and the road he terrorized became feared through all the land.

One day, the giant saw a lonely figure dressed like a hermit in a simple tunic. All he had with him was a sack of flour.

"I'm hungry," snarled the giant. "I'll have fresh bread from that wretch's flour this evening."

At once he leapt down from the rocks and threatened the man. "Give me the bag you are carrying, and any other treasure you have," he snarled.

The man stopped. He put the sack on the ground. "I have this flour," he said, "but it is something I have been given to share with a poor family who live on the other side of the mountains. I have only one other treasure."

"Show me what it is!" demanded the giant.

The man reached inside his tunic. "Look," he said, and he pulled out a plain wooden cross hanging on a cord around his neck. "This is the sign of my faith in Jesus Christ. Violent and angry people had him put to death on a cross of wood, but God who is greater than all evil raised him to life again. The treasure of my faith is knowing that the way of life is the way of gentleness and love."

Suddenly the giant felt as weak as a tiny baby. Tears began to trickle from the corners of his eyes.

"Take heart," said the hermit. "Let us make a loaf of bread from a little of this flour, and as we eat together I will tell you more."

So the giant learned to have faith in Jesus Christ, and the hermit showed him how to mend his life.

"Give up the life of a bandit," the hermit instructed him. "See how here in the valley the road passes through a river. It is easy to ford when the river is low, but whenever water rushes down from the mountains the

trickle becomes a flood. Then travellers easily lose their footing and many are swept away. Use your strength to help them cross in safety. They will love and respect you, and no doubt they will give you gifts to supply every need."

And so it was. A farmer came with a cartload of grain, and the giant guided his horse through the river. In return, he received two sacks of grain.

A merchant and his bodyguards came with gold in their pockets. The giant carried each of them through the water and received a purse full of coins.

A weaver came with bundles of cloth to take to market. The giant carried him and his load to safety. In return, he was sent a set of clothes.

Years passed. Then, one evening, a child came.

"Help me to cross," pleaded the child.

"I will, gladly," said the giant, "though it is not right for someone as young as you are to be out on the road alone."

"I have been sent by my father," came the reply, "and must return to him."

The giant nodded. Then he swung the child onto his shoulders and set off across the river.

Now, as he began the crossing, the river was only as deep as the giant's knees. But as he took another step, it seemed to rise, and, by the time he was in the middle of the river, a great torrent was flooding down from the mountains.

The child clung to the giant's shoulders, but with every step it seemed the child was growing heavier and heavier. The giant struggled against the swirling waters, almost losing his footing and bowing under the weight.

"Out of the goodness of your heart, give all your strength to keep me safe!" cried the child.

"I will," declared the giant, and with a great effort he planted one step more firmly, and then another, and then another.

At last they reached the other shore, and the giant set the child down on the path.

"Thank you," said the child—and then vanished. The giant rubbed his eyes. All through the night he wondered who the child was, and what the meeting had meant.

The next day, his friend the hermit came by and heard the tale.

"The child you bore was Jesus, the Christ-child," he explained, "and the weight that nearly overcame you was the weight of all the evil in the world, which Jesus came to carry away.

"And so from now on you will be called Christopher, Christ-bearer. Your story will be told, and it will bring strength and safety to all who travel this world and seek to do good in it."

The Golden Light

A Folk Tale

EVERY EVENING, a tiny golden light shone from high on the hill above the town.

"The nuns are at prayer in their church," said the townspeople.

As the nuns put out the candles before returning to their dormitory in the convent, they looked down at the sea of lights below them.

"The townspeople are enjoying themselves in one another's company," they smiled.

Every market day, two of the nuns would take a basket of produce to the town to sell: cheese and cakes, and herbs and honey. As the town clock chimed six, they would return, so as not to be late for their prayers in the church.

At the very edge of the town was one small house that seemed to crouch low among the weeds that twined around the door. Its window was cracked and the curtain hung in tatters.

"Have you ever seen a light in that house?" Sister Teresa asked, one evening in the autumn.

"I haven't," replied Sister Maria. "But in the summer, when the dark came later, I'm sure we sometimes saw an elderly lady peering from the window."

"If she lives alone, perhaps we should call on her," suggested Sister Teresa.

So they knocked on the door. The old woman who came to answer looked worried, and her fear made her angry.

"What do you want?" she snapped.

"We are nuns from the convent on the hill," the sisters replied. "We came because we are neighbors, even though it is some way from your door to ours."

The old woman hesitated. "Do you want to rest here a moment before you travel on?" she asked shyly. "I have nothing else to offer you."

"We must hurry to our prayers," said Sister Maria, but Sister Teresa, who was the older of the two, smiled.

"We would be delighted to accept your kindness," she said.

The two nuns entered her low cottage, which was grey with shadows.

"Do you live alone?" asked Sister Teresa.

The old woman began to tell her story. Her two sons had gone to a faraway country, and then her husband had died. Now she was all alone. Her only means of living were the things she could grow in her tiny patch of garden, and the money she received as, piece by piece, she sold anything of value that she had.

The woman sighed. "The only thing that is worth anything now is my lamp," she said. "It was a gift from my godmother when I was married. But I will need to sell it soon. Anyway, I cannot afford to light it—and I don't need to, being here on my own."

"You're not alone tonight," said Sister Teresa. "Promise

not to sell it. We will bring some oil to put in it next week, and we will sit together again."

"But what of prayers?" whispered Sister Maria.

"We will ask permission to stay longer, instead of hurrying to church," said Sister Teresa aloud.

And that is what happened. The woman seemed pleased to see them and smiled as golden light spilled into the room.

Then her face clouded over.

"I have let the lamp grow dull and black," she sighed. "And the corner where it sits is full of cobwebs."

"It does not matter for now," said Sister Teresa. "Let us share the cake we have brought. Next time we come we will admire how well you have polished the lamp."

The following week the sisters came again. The woman was waiting at the door for them.

Inside, the lamp was already lit, and the gold light made the brass sparkle. The table was scrubbed and the floor was swept.

"What a cosy welcome we have this week!" exclaimed Sister Teresa.

As the weeks went by, the woman grew happier, and as she began to chatter and laugh, she seemed to grow younger and stronger.

She cleaned her house from top to bottom.

She repaired the quilt that lay on the bed and found an untorn piece of fabric to hang as a curtain.

She collected fallen wood from the nearby copse and kept a small fire burning through the cold days.

In the spring, she began to clear her garden of weeds and sowed neat rows of vegetables and herbs. As she worked outdoors, she began to smile at other neighbors who passed by, and began visiting them.

She took bunches of herbs to market and earned a little money. "Enough for the things I need this winter…and the oil for my lamp," she smiled. "For now I have friends, and I will light the lamp every evening to welcome them." As she finished her sentence, she drew a sharp breath.

"But I hope you will still come, as you did last winter," she insisted.

"We will come a little earlier," said the nuns, "for we must return to our prayers, and you must have time for your friends. But every night you will be able to see our light shining, and we will see yours."

The Little Juggler

A Folk Tale

LONG AGO, in a little Italian town, the crowds were gathering.

"Look, here come the performers now!" cried the children. "There are jugglers and acrobats and people who do all kinds of magic."

The show began, and everyone was entranced. "See how the acrobats fly through air! They cannot be ordinary humans!"

"And look how that man conjures up objects from nowhere! Is it devils or angels who fly invisibly around his hands to place things there?"

But the star of the show was a young boy who could juggle. He juggled with a set of brightly painted balls. He juggled with hoops of gold and silver. In a moment of mischief he grabbed some pottery cups from a market stall and juggled with those.

Everyone laughed at the stallholder's fright. "My cups! My wares! You'll break them! I'll make you pay!"

But although the juggler threw them high in the air and then spun round in a merry dance, he caught every last one.

Everyone clapped in delight. And the same thing happened in the next town, and the next…everywhere the troupe of performers travelled.

The years went by, and the juggler grew more and more successful. He began to believe what the crowds said—that he was surely not a mere mortal, for his skills defied the laws of nature. He lived extravagantly and enjoyed spending the money he made.

But the day came when he awoke feeling wearier than usual. "I shall work less," he said to himself. And so he did, although he made less money.

Not only did he feel tired, but he found he was not as quick as he used to be. More than once he nearly failed to spin around quickly enough to catch the balls he had flung so high.

One day, he missed a catch.

The crowd was not forgiving. They booed more loudly than they had cheered. They talked in the market and in the inn of his mistake.

At his next performance he made another mistake…and another.

The leader of the troupe was kind—but he was also strict. "You have been successful for many years," he said. "But all of us grow older, and the skills of our youth are less sharp. It is time for you to find something else to do."

The little juggler found himself travelling alone along the road, looking for a new path to travel in life.

At night he sat and watched the moon and the glittering stars.

"The One who made the heavens is the greatest juggler of all," he sighed. "For the millions of stars follow the course that he directs, and he will never grow old and clumsy."

Then, in the dark of the night, the little juggler knew clearly what he would do. He would go to a monastery and serve God as a monk till the end of his days.

He found a monastery, and was given some time to see if the new life suited him.

It was not easy.

He was not used to kneeling in prayer. He was not used to hours of quiet. He could sing strongly enough, but he was not used to making his voice blend with that of others.

He began to feel that there was nothing he could do well.

One day, he was set the task of polishing the silverware which was used in the church. All around him the figures of saints and angels were gazing down.

"I used to entertain crowds as big as this and bigger," he said aloud.

The saints and angels seemed to smile.

Suddenly, the little juggler had an idea.

He ran to fetch his old juggling balls and returned to the church. "This is for you," he cried to the silent watchers.

For the first time in months, he began to juggle. Round and round the balls spun. High in the air they flew. The juggler felt once again the delight in his old skills.

"What do you think you're doing?" The voice of his superior echoed around the church. The juggler made one last wild throw.

The balls clattered to the floor. "This is no way for you to behave. This is the house of God," admonished the older man.

Ashamed, the little juggler made his apology and began to gather up the balls.

"Have you got them all?" questioned the older monk sharply.

"There is still one missing," replied the juggler, and he began to crawl about on all fours to see where it had rolled.

While he was looking, the abbot himself came by. He was told of the juggler's misdeed.

The abbot stood by gravely. Then he pointed upwards.

"Look!" he said. "I think I see the missing ball there."

They all craned their necks to look. High up near the ceiling was a statue of Mary cradling the infant Jesus. The baby's hand was outstretched, and it had caught the ball.

The abbot smiled. "It seems that the Lord Jesus has enjoyed your performance, and accepts your skill as a special gift to be used in his honor," he said to the juggler. "From this day forward, your service to our community will be to juggle for the joy of the Lord."

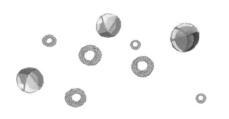

The Good Man of Assisi

A Tale of Saint Francis

LONG AGO, in Italy, there lived a man named Francis. He was born into a wealthy family, but as a young man he turned his back on riches and gave his life to living as Jesus taught. He travelled the land dressed in a simple tunic, looking for ways to help the poor and the needy. He walked gently among the animals, and called all things his brothers and his sisters.

One day, he came to a field where the herdsman was looking after a flock of goats. Among them tottered one tiny lamb, bleating

sadly for its mother. But its cries went unnoticed.

Francis felt sorry for the poor creature. "Look," he said to his companions. "See how meekly the lamb is walking among the goats. Listen to its cries. And yet it is left all on its own.

"The lamb makes me think of Jesus, who walked meekly on this earth among people who did not want to know him. He spoke his message, that all people should love God and one another, yet his words went unnoticed by many.

"Because of the love I have for Jesus, I want to take pity on that poor lamb. Let us pay the price for her and take her to a kinder place."

"We would like to do so," replied one of his companions, "but you know we have no money, for any that we are given we share with the poor."

While they were wondering what to do, a wealthy merchant came by. He stopped to greet Francis, for he knew what a good and saintly man he was. Hearing of the problem, he offered to buy the lamb.

Francis carried the creature gently, and those who saw him were touched and amused by his fondness for it.

In the next town, the leader of the church shook his head at the sight. "What will you do with the lamb?" he asked. "It will grow into a plump sheep, and you will not able to carry it with you then!"

Francis shrugged. "God will find a good way to solve the problem," he smiled.

And so it was. There was a convent close by, and as soon as the good nuns heard of the problem, they agreed to let the lamb come and graze in the meadow.

"Be sure to take good care of the creature," Francis insisted.

"We will keep it safe," the nuns replied.

A year went by, and a second. Then, one day, Francis received a large package.

Inside was a new tunic, neatly woven in the warmest wool. With it came a message: "We have made you this tunic from the wool we have sheared from your sheep," it said. "Your kindness inspired us to greater kindness...to your lamb, to you and to all in need."

The Fisher Princess

The Tale of Elizabeth of Hungary

LONG AGO, in Hungary, there lived a little princess named Elizabeth. When she was very young, she was sent to live with the ruling family of another country.

"She will grow up as a friend to our son Ludwig," the family had agreed. "As soon as she is old enough, the two will marry."

Ludwig was often busy learning to be a soldier, and for entertainment the little girl was left exploring, accompanied only by a servant.

"There seem to be a lot of poor people here," she announced one day when she was out in the city. "Doesn't anyone take care of them?"

"That's not a problem for a princess to worry about," said the servant.

"In my old home I was taught that it is," said Elizabeth firmly. "Is that not what our Christian faith teaches?"

She opened her purse and began giving coins to the beggars who sat around the market square.

News of what she had done reached Ludwig's parents. "That is no way for the future princess to behave," they fumed.

From that time on, the people at the court watched Elizabeth more closely. "She doesn't often wear the fine robes that were

made for her," they whispered. "She prefers to dress in plain clothes as she roams around among the common people."

"And how dare she give away so much money," muttered the Chancellor. "Ludwig's family have hoarded their wealth carefully. It should not be squandered on beggars."

"And why does she linger so long in church?" sighed the priest. "Does anyone need to spend so long at prayer after Mass?"

Only the young Ludwig remained loyal. "Elizabeth is my best friend," he said. "Let her do as she thinks right."

Although his parents were beginning to whisper about finding a more suitable bride, Ludwig insisted that, at the right time, he and Elizabeth be married.

It was a splendid occasion, and all the people in the kingdom cheered for their new princess whom they had grown to love. They were delighted when she had her first child, and then a second and a third.

Although she was busy being a mother, she did not forget her people. She arranged for hospitals to be set up, where the poor and the sick could be cared for. When she had the time, she went in person to help in whatever way she could.

The people at the royal court were shocked. "She may fall ill herself," they hissed.

"Or worse, she may bring some disease to the palace that will kill her husband," scowled one.

"Or harm the children," muttered another.

"Let her do what she thinks is right," insisted Ludwig. "My kingdom is a better place for all her kindness."

So the courtiers sighed and waited. When famine struck the country and Elizabeth asked Ludwig to open the royal granaries to the poor, they knew it was useless to protest.

"We simply won't talk to her," they agreed among themselves.

"She must be daft in the head," they comforted themselves.

"Perhaps she'll starve herself," they began to dream as they watched her eat smaller and simpler meals, just as the poor had to do.

Then, when Elizabeth was expecting her fourth child, bad news came. "There is a war in another country," sighed Ludwig, "and I feel it is right for me to go and fight."

Elizabeth wept. "I fear you will never return," she said, hugging him close as they said a tearful goodbye.

The months went by, and Elizabeth's baby was born. Then the news she had feared arrived: Ludwig had died of the plague.

Elizabeth spent the next day weeping, and the next. While she sat in sorrow, the courtiers were whispering, "Now is the time to get rid of her."

Within a short time, Elizabeth was banished from the palace. All she was allowed to take with her was her newborn child.

As night fell and the child began to wail, Elizabeth felt close to despair. "Where can I stay, oh, where can I stay?" she wept. "I have been sent out into the wildest country, far from anyone who knows me."

At last, Elizabeth came to a tumbledown farmhouse. The people who lived there looked like ruffians, but they took pity on the woman with her child.

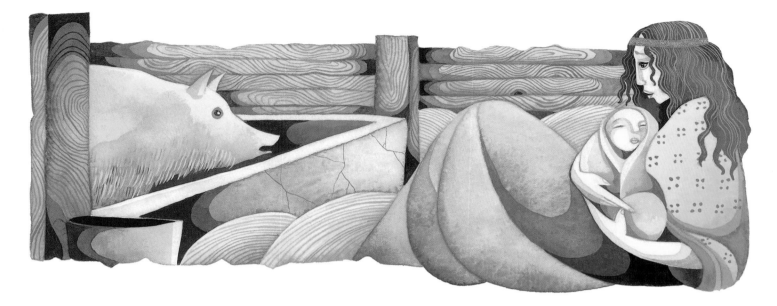

"The pig house is empty," they explained. "It's well built—and it's a place you can make your own…though it smells a bit."

Elizabeth was grateful for their help. "If this is where God has let me be sent, then it is here that I shall find ways to live for God," she told herself.

The gentle way she endured her poverty soon became the talk of the land. Soon, the gossip was about the wickedness of those who had driven her from the palace.

"We must take notice of the people's discontent," said the chancellor one day. "If we continue to leave that wretched Elizabeth living in a pig house, they will turn against us, and we could end up the losers."

Enquiries were made, and a cottage was found for Elizabeth to live in. "Live here quietly," she was warned, "and stay out of our way."

Elizabeth smiled. "Certainly," she said. She spent her days spinning wool, for which she earned a little money to buy what she needed. In the evenings, she visited the poor and those in

need. In the quiet of the morning she would rise early to pray...
and sometimes she went to sit by a quiet stream to enjoy the
beauty of the early morning world. There, she cast a line to catch
fish, and what she caught she sold so she could give money to
those who were poorer than herself.

And so she lived for a few years until the hardship of her life
drove her to the grave.

"It is a shame she never knew how to be a proper princess,"
sighed the people at court.

"It is a wonder that she was not born an angel," marvelled the
ordinary people.

"Then let us remember her as a saint," they agreed.

The Three Trees

A Folk Tale

LONG AGO, on a hillside, stood three young trees. In the bright daytime they bravely spread their leaves to the golden sun, and in the night they whispered in the quiet breeze.

One night, under the silver stars, they spoke to one another of their dreams.

"My wood is smooth and golden," said the first tree. "When I grow up, I want to be made into a chest for the finest treasure."

"My wood is hard and strong," said the second. "When I grow up, I want to be made into a warship that will carry a mighty king."

The third tree bowed in the wind. "I just want to stay here," she said, "and I want to grow tall and lovely so that people who look at me will lift their eyes to heaven."

The changing seasons came and went and the trees all grew tall.

Then the day came when three woodcutters climbed the hill.

One looked up at the first tree. "This tree has the fine timber I need," he said. With his axe, he felled it to the ground. "Perhaps my dream is about to come true," she smiled.

Another stood at the base of the second tree. "This one has the good strong wood I am looking for," he said. With his axe, he felled it to the ground. "Surely my dream is beginning," laughed the tree.

The third woodcutter stood at the base of the one remaining tree. "Any kind of timber is good enough for me," he muttered. He lifted his axe. "And my dream is surely over," wept the third tree as she crashed down.

A carpenter took the wood from the first tree. He measured it carefully and fashioned it with skill, but all he made was a simple wooden trough. A farmer bought it and filled it with hay for his animals.

"So I am not a treasure chest," sighed the tree sadly. "My dream is over."

Then, one night, when the stars seemed to dance in the nighttime sky, the tree heard gentle voices in the animal shed. A man and a woman were sheltering there. The man fetched clean straw to put in the trough and spread a blanket. There, the woman laid her newborn baby.

All at once, the tree knew that she was holding treasure, the greatest treasure in all the world.

A shipbuilder took the wood from the second tree. He measured it carefully and fashioned it with skill, but all he made was a plain fishing boat. Night after night, rough and cheerful men sailed it on a windswept lake and emptied into it their catch of slithering, smelly fish.

"So I am not the vessel that will carry a king to victory," sighed the tree. "My dream is over."

One night, the wildest of storms swept the lake. The waves crashed against the boat and threatened to smash the timbers. The

water poured over the sides and drove the craft deeper and deeper into the angry swirling waters.

"Help! We will surely drown," shouted the fishermen in terror.

They woke the one man who was sleeping on the floor of the boat and pleaded with him to help battle with the storm.

The man smiled and stood up. "Hush," he said to the wind. "Be still," he said to the waves.

At once there was calm, and the tree knew that the man who had spoken was the greatest king in all the world.

The third tree was carried to a woodyard. There she was hacked
into thick beams and left in the open, seemingly forgotten. The tree
felt the heat of summer and the cold of winter, but she knew her
dream was dead and gone.

One day, she heard shouting. Soldiers had marched into the
woodyard. Roughly they hauled her out. They loaded her onto a
cart and carried her away.

She felt herself being loaded onto someone's shoulders, and
carried through a jeering, angry crowd to the top of a bare and

rocky hill. There a man was laid upon her, and nails driven through his hands and feet. She was lifted upright and placed in the ground in the shape of a cross, where the man hung until he died.

His body was taken away. There was nighttime and daytime as before.

Then, on the third day, the sun rose and awakened all the world to joy. News was whispered on the breeze and blazed across the sky. By the power of heaven's love, the man who had died was alive again.

Then the third tree knew that her dream had come true. For ever after people would turn to look at her, and think of heaven.

The Easter Fire

A Legend of Saint Patrick

WINTER LINGERED ON sullenly in ancient Ireland. The lowering sky was heavy with clouds, and a chill drizzle drifted in the wind.

"We shall make our camp here," said Patrick to his companions, "at the foot of the hill of Tara."

"Are you sure that your plan is worth the risk?" Patrick's friends asked him. "We can see the preparations the king is making for the great fire festival. When all the fires in the land are dimmed tonight, it is forbidden on pain of death to light another before the king lights the ritual fire."

Patrick shrugged his shoulders. "That is the old superstition," he said. "It is God who is lord of the seasons. Spring will come because of God's goodness; magic rituals achieve nothing."

From high on the hill came the sound of shouting and soldiers clattering their weapons. Patrick's friends asked another question: "Do you not fear the king's anger? He has great power on his side."

"Nothing is greater than the power of God," explained Patrick, "and nothing shows God's power more than the news we celebrate at dawn."

Patrick and his companions finished their preparations and put out their fire before going to sleep.

From his castle on the hill, the king had been watching. "It's that meddling Patrick, the one who preaches about Jesus," he grumbled to his soldiers. "Watch him carefully. And, most of all, be ready to go and get rid of him if he disregards the traditions of the festival."

The night wore on: all over the land, the fires were put out. The moon was swathed in clouds, and the stars could not be seen. Darkness ruled the land.

Then, at last, a small bird woke and warbled.

Down in the valley, a great fire blazed out. "Today we celebrate our belief that Jesus Christ is risen," cried Patrick. "God welcomes us all into heaven's glorious light!"

"Traitor," shouted the king. "Death to Patrick!"

The king and his soldiers rode out, wild and savage, their gleaming weapons at the ready.

Patrick and his companions stood in the golden light, saw them coming and turned to go. "After them!" screamed the king. Then he stopped, reining his horse in and wiping his eyes.

"Can you see where they went?" asked the soldier at his side.

For suddenly Patrick and his companions were nowhere to be seen. Instead, all the king and his soldiers could see was a group of deer, leaping and bounding into the forest.

The king shook his head. He looked around, anxious and alarmed. "Perhaps I need to think again," he said. "Perhaps the power that protects Patrick is greater than the old magic." He put away his sword. "Let us not oppose Patrick's God," he said.

As he spoke, the first rays of the dawn light showed in the eastern sky.

The Slave Girl and Her Master

The Tale of Bakhita

WHEN BAKHITA WAS a little girl, she loved to play in the African sunshine, exploring among the tall grasses, juggling with pebbles from the dry riverbed, and running so fast that the air whistled past her as if there were a wind. "What a wonderful place to live in," she laughed to herself.

In the evening, her mother used to sing her to sleep with a lullaby, a song that told her over and over again how much she was loved.

"You have so much, my little one," her mother used to say. "That is why I called you Bakhita, the fortunate one."

One terrible day, Bakhita's fortune blew away. A gang of raiders swept down on her village and carried her away to be sold as a slave. She was condemned to working all her waking hours. Sometimes she was outdoors, in blazing sun and freezing cold; sometimes she was indoors, in stifling rooms and windowless basements. Often she was beaten and treated cruelly.

When she was just fourteen, she was bought by a family who treated her kindly. They took her to a country across the blue sea where the wind blew among the olive trees and grapes ripened in the sunshine.

"Your principal duty is to take care of our baby daughter, Mimmina," her new mistress explained. "You are to tidy and clean for her, do her laundry, prepare her meals and also watch over her carefully. I am sure you will be able to amuse her with simple games and songs too."

Bakhita had never enjoyed her work so much. As she watched Mimmina grow, she remembered her own childhood and the days full of happiness and sunshine. She remembered her mother's lullaby, and the meaning of her name. "Once again, I am a fortunate one," she sighed.

The day came when Mimmina was old enough to go to school. She was sent to a convent school in the beautiful city of Venice, and Bakhita went with her.

The nuns were very kind. They treated Bakhita with the same respect and gentleness that they showed to everyone. They told her of their faith in the God who made the world and who, in ancient days, gave people laws to guide them.

"The laws of God were given to a people who had suffered terrible slavery," explained the nuns. "God sent a leader named Moses to lead them to freedom, for God wants all people to live in freedom and dignity."

Bakhita marvelled at the teaching. "So God is like the Master of everyone in the world," she said. "Only he is a master who gives people their freedom."

The nuns agreed.

That night, when Mimmina was asleep, Bakhita looked up at the stars wheeling across the night sky. "Surely God wants me to be free too. Then only God will be my true Master for ever," she dreamed.

Only a few months passed before Mimmina's family announced their plan to return to Africa. "But I want to stay here and serve the true Master," Bakhita pleaded.

Her mistress was angry and upset. "We have treated you well," she scolded. "I am so disappointed that you are not willing to serve Mimmina for ever."

The nuns heard of the argument. "If Bakhita chooses to stay and serve God as her Master, she is welcome to come and stay with us," they told her mistress. "You know that here in Italy it is against the law to own a slave...so Bakhita is not a slave but only a servant."

Bakhita claimed her freedom. She was baptized into the faith she had learned from the nuns, and was given the name of Josephine. When she was a grown woman she decided to become a nun at the convent that had first made her welcome.

"Here I can stay and serve God my Master," she sang happily. "I can cook and clean and sew and mend, and all the time I can say prayers to God."

And so she did. So eagerly did she serve her God that the holiness of heaven seemed to shine through her. Wherever she was, she spread a gentleness and joy to everyone.

As an old lady, she eventually became so ill that she could not leave her wheelchair. No more could she labor as she had done since she was young.

One day, a bishop of the church asked what she was able to do in the long hours she had to spend in her wheelchair. "What do I do? Exactly what you are doing —the will of God," she replied brightly.

The Ploughman Saint

The Legend of Saint Isidore

WHEN ISIDORE WAS a little boy, his father taught him to plough.

"You must drive a straight furrow," the older man explained. "Then the one you drive next to it will also be straight, and the next, and the next. In this way, you will prepare the land well for sowing, and the rain and the sun from heaven will give you a good harvest."

Isidore listened carefully and did his best. The village priest stood watching. "A simple job that you do for God is the greatest thing you can ever do," the priest said encouragingly. "So when you plough, pray to God for help, and set your eyes straight ahead, as one who is looking to heaven."

Isidore took the advice to heart. As a young man, he was taken on as a farmworker by the wealthy man who owned all the land in that part of Spain. "He is a good worker," approved the farm manager, "and deserves one of our small cottages, so that he and the girl he plans to marry can make their home there."

Isidore carried his bride, Maria, over the threshold of the cottage. "You are the dear companion who will walk with me all the way to heaven," he laughed.

So the couple grew in love for one another and for all the world.

"No one ploughs as well as Isidore," said a neighbor. "He says it is because he prays to God as he follows the team of oxen up and down the land."

"Well God has certainly answered his prayers," commented another. "Yesterday, I watched him on the hillside...and there I saw angels leading the oxen, guiding their steps and urging them to keep up a good pace."

"Maria is always so busy in her garden," said a housewife, as she travelled with her friends to market. "She has onions and leeks and peas and beans...and a hive of bees and a pen of chickens. I wonder her husband isn't fatter with the wonderful meals she must be able to cook."

"Oh, but haven't you seen who comes to supper with them?" commented another. "Her husband is too generous, and invites the poor to come and share their meal. I have heard that he will not eat till he is sure that they have had their fill."

"I thank God for blessing us with good harvests," said Isidore to himself as he walked along the frosted track. "I still have this sackful of corn left to be ground into flour, though the winter is perilously long this year."

As he walked along he heard the twittering of birds in the bare trees. He looked up. "Are the fields and hedges bare of food?" he called to them. For answer came a mournful chorus.

"Come, there is something here for you," said Isidore and, swinging his sack to the ground, opened it and let half the golden grain spill onto the ground. The birds swooped down and began to gobble it happily.

Isidore carried his half sack to the mill. The miller was busy, but he called down to Isidore that he would deal with his sack of grain within the week.

When Isidore returned, he found a bulging sack of flour ready for him to collect.

"Surely that is too much," said Isidore. "My sack was only half full when I left it here."

"I've only given you what you brought," explained the miller. "But I remember well that there was a nice full sack waiting for me after you left."

Isidore shrugged. "If you are sure this is for me to take, then I will do so gladly, for there will be more to share through the cold days."

In this way, Isidore and Maria passed their life together, caring for one another and for everyone they met. One evening, Isidore was driving his team of oxen back from a day's ploughing.

"Well done, good creatures," he called. "This is the best day's ploughing we have ever done together."

Then he rubbed his eyes. Angels appeared before him. Some unhitched the animals and led them to the barn. Others pushed the plough to the shelter of a shed. Two others took Isidore by the hand. "Come," they said. "Maria is not at home. She is waiting for you in heaven. Let us go straight there."

In this way Isidore left his earthly life and went to be with God in heaven.

Poor Little Rich Girl

A Folk Tale

SUSANNA WAS A merchant's daughter, and she was both rich and pretty. Since she was a tiny baby, servants had looked after her who had always told her that she was adorable. But, although she was pretty, having her own way made her ill-tempered and selfish.

When she grew older, she began to see that she was not as popular as she had imagined. While the other girls danced together, she was left alone.

"What is the matter with them all?" she complained to her old nurse the next morning. "I want to snap my fingers and make them like me."

"Oh, if you want a change like that, then you had better go and see the wise woman who lives on the mountain," advised the grey-haired servant.

"I shall send one of the stable lads with a message," replied Susanna. "I am sure that for a bag of coins she will tell me how to get what I want."

The messenger went, but returned at sunset with the bag of coins still full.

"The wise woman said that if you want to know how to make people invite you to join their dancing, then you must go to her yourself," he explained. "And she said that you must go on foot."

Susanna frowned and pouted, and for a week she refused to go. Then she began to see that while she did nothing, there would be no change. "I can see I shall have to go myself," she sulked, and she ordered the servants to prepare what she needed for the journey: smart little boots of the finest leather, a warm woollen cloak and a bag of food.

She set off in the early morning, through the streets of the town and on to the track that led into the hills.

As she walked on, she began to feel her smart boots pinching her toes. "They must have been made too small,"

she complained to herself. She soon came to a cottage where an old woman was sitting on a bench by her front door.

"Oh, my feet are hurting so badly," Susanna exclaimed, sitting down beside her. "Yet I have to walk all the way to the wise woman who lives on the mountain."

The old woman looked at Susanna and she looked at her boots.

"I only have these battered shoes," said the woman, "but they have stretched so much over the years that they have grown too big for me. They might fit you better than the pair you have on."

"I suppose I could try them," she said. To her amazement, the old shoes fitted her very well. So she gave her boots to the woman and travelled on.

As Susanna climbed higher towards the mountain, the air grew colder and the wind began to blow her cloak around. Then the grey clouds gathered and rain began to fall in great, heavy drops.

Susanna ran on and spied a woodsman's cottage among the trees.

"Thank goodness there is shelter," she cried, running under the porch where the woodsman stood. "I would be wet through with just a woollen cloak."

The woodsman looked at her. "You'd be better with the piece of canvas I have on the bed. But my wife is sick and she would have nothing to keep her warm if I gave it to you."

"Might you exchange it for my cloak?" asked Susanna hopefully.

"If you wish," agreed the woodsman. He brought a ragged square of canvas for her to wrap around her shoulders, and he took her cloak gratefully and hugged it.

Susanna trudged on, hour after hour, nibbling from her bag of food as she went.

As she reached the higher slopes, she came to a shepherd's cottage and heard a woman crying.

The woman explained that her child was sick and she had nothing to give him to eat until her husband returned from town. "That will be the day after tomorrow," she sobbed, "and the child is already weak."

Susanna opened her bag. "See, I have fresh bread, soft and sweet," she said, "and a portion of butter too. Please have it and make your child well."

The woman was full of thanks, and wished Susanna well in her journey.

It was almost nightfall when Susanna reached the top of the mountain where the wise woman lived. Wearily, she went to knock on the door of the little hut. There was no answer. She waited and waited, but no one came.

"Oh, I have come so far—and all for nothing!" Susanna wept, then she anxiously tested the door to the hut. Finding it open, she went inside to shelter for the night. To her surprise, she found that the bed was spread with freshly cut heather, and on the top lay a message: "I have said my prayers for you, and you will find that your journey will bring the change you want."

Too tired to care any more, Susanna lay down to rest for the night. The following morning she set off for home as the sun rose.

When she reached the shepherd's hut, she found the mother by the front door, laughing with her son: "He is so much better," she called to Susanna, and Susanna realized she had never once felt hungry since sharing her food.

When she reached the woodsman's cottage, she saw him standing with his wife in the clearing. "I slept so well for being warm I feel strong enough to get up after many days in bed," said the woman.

Susanna realized that the rain had not chilled her since she had had the canvas for shelter.

When she reached the old woman's house, she found the woman ironing.

"I'm just getting my best clothes ready to go to my niece's wedding tomorrow," she explained. "I was hoping I might be able to keep your lovely boots a little longer, for they are so much nicer than my shoes, and they fit me well."

"Oh, keep them for ever," said Susanna. "The ones you gave me have been just right for the journey."

"They were good shoes once," said the woman. "I wore them for working, for walking…and most of all for dancing. Although they are so old, I'm sure you will find you can dance well in them."

Susanna's face lit up. "I'll try!" she said.

And with that she danced all the way to the town, and she felt as good as new.

A group of girls she knew saw her smiling and clapping and skipping and twirling. "Well done, well done!" they called. "Come and dance with us."

And Susanna did

The River

A Folk Tale

FOR AS LONG as anyone could remember, the People had lived by the river.

The river provided everything.

It gave water for drinking, water for washing and water for the crops.

It teemed with fish that were good for eating.

It carried their boats down to the great city by the sea, and yet its gentle current always allowed them to return upstream to their home.

Its banks and its shallows were a lovely place to play.

All of the People's traditions—their stories, their songs and their beliefs—were centered on the river. Each year, they held a great festival in celebration of it, with joyful parties held on brightly lit boats that danced on the moonlit ripples.

"Hooray for our river," cried the children.

One year, the river was a little lower than they had hoped.

"Each season is different," the old people nodded. "The last months have seen little rain, but our river will never fail."

But the river continued to fall.

"Unless the flow returns to normal, we will have to be careful how much water we use for our crops," said the men.

"And the water we have is more bitter than usual, and not so clean," complained the women.

"And the river is no longer a nice place to play," sighed the children.

That year, the festival was not a success. There was so little water that the carnival boats were scarcely floating. No one shouted hooray.

A month later, the river bed was almost dry.

The children who gathered by the river bank grew sulky. "What can we do now?" they asked one another.

Then a girl spoke. "I know," she said. "Let's go and find the river!"

All the children jumped to their feet. "Yes, let's go," they said. And they raced off to tell their families of the great plan.

"But you have no idea what kind of journey you face," warned their parents. "Who can tell what has happened: you may walk and walk, and all for nothing."

"If the river is still flowing, then it will flow here," grumbled the grandparents. "Here is where it belongs. Our stories say so. Our songs say so. We say so too."

"But we can at least go and look," argued the children.

At last it was agreed, and a great party of young people set off to find the river that gave them life.

The way was long and hard: up the mountain tracks and into the blue horizon. But at last, after many days' marching, they crossed

a mountain pass, and what they saw dazzled their eyes: a waterfall so pure and beautiful it seemed it must come from heaven itself, its spray glittering in the sunlight.

"Look," they cried. "There is the river! A fall of rock has made it change course, but now it is tumbling into another valley, and a new land is green with meadows and bright with flowers."

Joyfully they returned home.

"Good news," they said. "The river is flowing in a new direction. We can make for ourselves a new home on the banks of the river that gives us life."

"But here is your home—and our home too," said the parents.

"And this is where our people's homes have always been and must always be," said the old people.

"But we cannot stay here without the river," said the girl who had first had the idea of going to find it. She looked around. All the people had gathered to hear of their journey of discovery, but now they were not wanting to listen to what was true.

"We cannot stay here," she said again. Then, in her mind, she saw again the great waterfall she had glimpsed. She spoke again. "We must be bold enough to follow wherever it is that the water of life flows down from heaven."

Her words fell into an anxious silence. The people looked at her, fearful and hostile.

Then her own grandmother stood up, straightening herself as she gripped the stick she used for walking.

"I shall always love this place and the traditions of the old days," she announced. "But if the river has moved, then I will go to find it in what will be my new home."

And so it was that the People moved to where the water of heaven flowed to bless them all.

The Monk and the Mice

A Tale of Martin de Porres

HUNDREDS OF YEARS AGO, in a monastery in Peru, there lived a great colony of mice.

Some lived near the hearth in the prior's room, where a roaring log fire kept them warm when it was cold.

Some lived behind the panels in the monks' dormitory where, during the day, they would sneak onto the beds and nibble away pieces of blanket with which to line their nests.

Like all mice everywhere, they were quick and clever at hiding, but they made life miserable for the monks.

· 75 ·

At last, the monks could stand it no more. "We must find a way to get rid of these pests," exclaimed the prior. "Indeed, we will try every way."

"Let's get a cat to hunt them," suggested one monk.

"Let's set a trap to snare them," said another.

"Let's sprinkle poison," said a third.

"Let's do all these things," agreed the prior.

But one monk held up his hand. "Wait a moment," he said.

"Do you have something to add to the plan, Martin?" asked the prior.

"I do," he replied. "I have had many pleasant meetings with our mouse friends. They are quite aware of how much they depend on us. I am sure if I told them that we would rather they lived a little

further away, we could come to a good arrangement."

The prior frowned, but some of the younger monks cheered. "Give it a try, Martin," they urged.

So the prior gave his permission.

Martin went to the kitchen, where a young mouse was scampering by with a lump of cheese. Gravely, Martin asked him to give the message that the chief mice from all over the monastery should gather in the kitchen for a meeting with him.

When they had all arrived, Martin spoke.

"There is a widespread feeling that you should not be living in the monastery buildings with us," he explained. "God created you animals of the wild, and I think you could make for yourselves cosy homes in the garden."

"Maybe," said the eldest of the mice, "but we are so many that it would be hard for us all to find food. Your fields and gardens grow good crops, but you harvest them very carefully."

"You are right," agreed Martin. "I myself am willing to bring you extra food from our stores. Next year, we will leave a bigger share of the harvest for you."

So it was agreed. The prior was amazed as the mice scurried happily down the stairs and along the passageways out of the monastery.

And thereafter, the monks and the mice lived in peace.

The Secret Giftbringer

A Legend of Saint Nicholas

IT WAS A DISMAL winter's day in the bustling town of Myra. The sleet was making a blanket of slush in the winding cobbled streets.

Three sisters were on their way home, carrying with them the few coppers they had begged that day.

"Oh, let's wait a moment," said the youngest. "Here comes a wedding procession. I do so want to see what the bride is wearing."

"Her dress is lovely," sighed the second, "and yet I would be glad to be married in these old rags."

"But it will never be," added the eldest, wiping away a tear, "for Father has told us that he has no money to pay for a dowry."

"Does that really mean that no family will want their son to marry one of us?" asked the youngest.

"It certainly does," answered the middle sister grimly.

"The only thing we have left to sell is ourselves," added the eldest bitterly.

At that, the three of them turned away from the crowded street where the wedding guests jostled happily and slipped towards an alley that led to the poorer part of town.

The Bishop of Myra was among the crowd and he smiled at the girls as they passed him.

"Do you think you will be getting married soon?" he asked in a kindly way.

The girls shook their heads. "Father has no money to pay for a dowry," they explained.

The bishop's face clouded over with sadness, and he stood watching the girls as they made their way back home.

The house they entered was a poor, single-storeyed shack. They kept the shutters closed in the wintry weather for there was nothing in the windows to prevent the cold wind from whistling through. From the

chimney spiralled a thin curl of smoke from the turf fire they had kept burning slowly through the day.

"My feet are wet through," shivered the youngest sister as they kicked off their shoes by the hearth.

"And mine are so cold," said the middle sister.

"But we can leave our shoes by the hearth and hang our stockings from the hooks that hold the fire irons," sighed the eldest. "At least we may start tomorrow a little warmer than we end today."

So they made themselves a little more comfortable in the dim light of the fire, waiting until their father returned. He was angry and dejected from another day in which he had found no work. Together, they ate their supper of bread and soup, hardly daring to think what misery the next day might bring. As the fire slipped lower, they went to bed.

Meanwhile the bishop had gone to join the wedding guests at their feast. His mind was still on the plight of the three sisters. Oh dear, he thought to himself. Poor girls who cannot afford to be married are often lured into the worst of jobs.

"Oh dear," he said to himself, as he sat at the wedding feast watching the rich food and drink that was being consumed so lavishly. "It is not right that some people have so much and others so little."

The father of the bride was in a generous mood that evening. "Ah, Nicholas," he said, as he caught sight of the bishop. "Thank you so much for performing the wedding ceremony today. I wanted to give you some small token of thanks for all your help and kindness," and he pressed a small leather purse of money into the old man's hands.

"A wedding is such a joyful event, is it not?" he said enthusiastically as he sauntered off to greet other guests.

"Indeed it is," said Nicholas, as he felt the weight of coins in the bag.

Around midnight, Nicholas slipped away from the feast and hurried to the shack where the sisters lived. The place was completely dark, and the door locked.

Then an idea struck him. An outer stairway of the house next door ran so close to the little hovel that a person could step from it onto the roof.

"And from there," said Nicholas, as he clambered across the tiles, "I can reach the chimney. There is so little smoke coming from it I am sure the coins will come to no harm in whatever fire there is left."

Laughing to himself, he tipped the purse of coins down the chimney and hurried away as quickly as he could.

In the morning, the youngest daughter awoke and went to fetch her stockings.

"Oh!" she exclaimed. "A gold coin has appeared from nowhere in my stocking."

The middle sister came to see. She grabbed her own stockings. "There is a coin in mine too," she said, "and look, more coins have rolled into our shoes."

"And there are coins in among the ashes as well," said the eldest sister, frowning with puzzlement and laughing at the same time.

Their father came to join in the merriment, and together they added up the gift.

"Well, I'm sure I will have no trouble talking to some of my old friends about who might make lovely brides for their sons," he smiled. "A gift has come as if from heaven itself and will bring us many blessings."

Somewhere in another part of town, Bishop Nicholas watched the sun rise. He laughed as he thought of the delight there would be in the house where the three sisters lived. "I hope the family is happier now," he said. "For my gift was given in love, and I hope that the love will spread far and wide."

The Fourth Wise Man

A Christmas Legend

ACROSS THE DESERT the wise men were riding…riding their camels through the dark of the night.

"See, the star is leading us!" cried the first.

"Leading us to a king," agreed the second.

"The king of heaven and earth," added the third.

There was a fourth man with them. "I wish I was as wise as my companions," he said to himself. "Then I would have known more about the reason for our journey before we set off."

"The gift I bring is hidden in my saddlebag," whispered the first.

"The gift I bring is strapped to my belt," answered the second.

"The gift I bring is sewn among the folds of my tunic," added the third.

The fourth man looked sad. "I have not yet found a gift worthy of the king," he sighed. "I am still looking."

"My gift is gold, for a king who is powerful," proclaimed the first.

"My gift is frankincense, for a king whose prayers will rise to God in heaven," announced the second.

"My gift is myrrh, for a king who will be famous in life and yet more famous in death," declared the third.

The fourth man lowered his eyes. "I don't even know what gift I would choose," he sighed.

So the four men travelled on through the night and continued their journey for many days and many nights.

At last, the star that led them hung still in the night sky. Below it was a humble dwelling.

"This is an unusual place to find a king," noted the first man.

"But the star clearly shows that it is the right place," replied the second.

"So let us go in and present our gifts," said the third.

The fourth man waited outside. "I may as well fetch water for the camels," he said to himself. "I have not found a gift for the one who is within."

He went to the well and drew a bucketful of water. It was heavy, and he set it down on the ground for a moment.

Then he saw something wonderful. He bent closer.

"The star," he said. "The star that is in the sky is also in my old and battered bucket."

He gazed in delight for a moment. And then he laughed aloud.

"This is what I shall take the king," he said, "a reflection of the light from the heavens."

And by a miracle, the star kept on shining in the bucket of water to make the child-king smile.

Grandfather's Boat

A Folk Tale

MARISA LIVED WITH her mother and her grandfather in a little cottage overlooking the sea.

Her grandfather was a fisherman, and his little boat with its brown sail bobbed in the waters of the harbor.

Sometimes her grandfather worked close to the shore, and Marisa loved to watch the little boat as it wound among the rocks and the inlets of the bay.

Sometimes her grandfather went out as evening was falling. Marisa loved to watch as the boat sailed off into the red gold light. Then she would go to her warm bed, happy in the thought that, as the sun rose behind the hills, she would see the boat's brown sail returning in pale dawn light.

Sometimes her grandfather went off for many days. Then, Marisa and her mother would go down to the edge of the pier to wave him a long goodbye as the drifting tide carried his boat into the mistiness of the horizon. There the boat seemed to sink into the vastness until only the tip of the mast could be seen.

Then the mast itself would disappear, and Marisa and her mother would be left alone together.

"He will return," her mother always promised. Sometimes she knew for sure on which tide he would return, and on those days Marisa would run to the top of the hill behind her house, watching until the tip of the mast appeared on the horizon.

She would cry, "Grandfather is coming, Grandfather is coming." Then with her mother she would run to the end of the pier to wave as the brown sail fluttered ever nearer and at last they could see her grandfather's smiling face once again.

Other times, the days would go by, and Marisa's mother would grow more worried. "It is the time of year for storms," she used to explain, "and Grandfather may be delayed for who knows how long."

But Marisa still waited to watch for his return. "If his trip has been frightening, he will be even more eager to see us," she would say.

She learned to recognize the moment when the tide was flooding in that was most likely to bring a boat into the harbor. Then she would go and watch.

Sometimes she would have a week of waiting and watching, and sometimes two…but the moment always came when the mast appeared and her grandfather returned.

"I sometimes wish that you wouldn't go away to sea and leave us alone," Marisa told her grandfather after one journey that had kept him away for many days.

"You will have your wish," sighed the old man. "I am not as strong as I used to be, and I dare not travel as far as I have done. From now on I will not go far…out and back within the day, when the tide is right."

At first, Marisa was happy, because she had more time with her grandfather. Then she began to see that he was growing more tired and frail every day, and wanted to stay close to the house.

"Will you not go out to the sea ever again?" asked Marisa anxiously.

"The only boat I shall sail on now is the one that takes me into the great beyond," he smiled.

Marisa pleaded with him. "Don't go! Don't ever go!" she cried.

"It is the journey I have lived for," he said quietly. "I have explored this world all I want to, and now I long to find a new one."

Not many days later, Marisa's grandfather died. The bell in the village church rang out solemnly as he was buried in the churchyard, overlooking the sea.

"Goodbye, Grandfather," Marisa whispered to the dark earth.

Then she ran alone to the end of the pier.

"Goodbye, Grandfather," she shouted to the fast running tide. "Goodbye and goodbye."

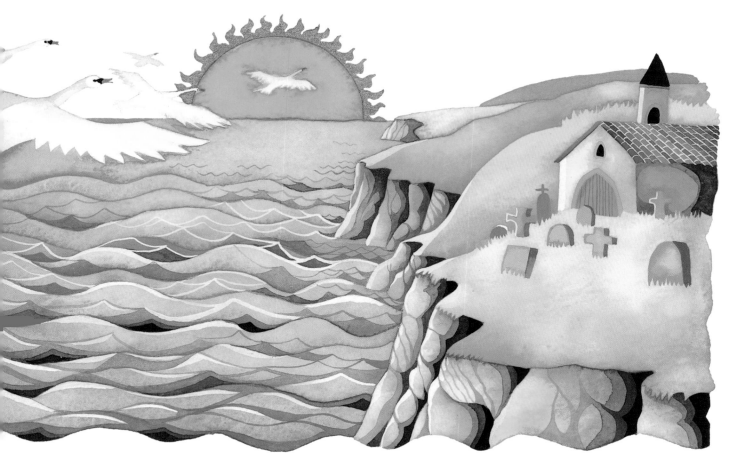

As the waters ebbed away from the shore, she waited for as long as it had ever taken Grandfather's boat to dip below the far horizon. Her mother came and stood beside her.

"So he is gone from our sight," she sighed. "But I do believe that on some far shore, in some new land, someone is watching him arrive."

About the Stories

The Cinderella Saint

There are obvious similarities between the story of Saint Germaine and Cinderella: the good and kind daughter is wickedly treated by her stepfamily but finally gets the fair reward she deserves. However, for Saint Germaine the "happily ever after" is found not by marrying a handsome prince but by dying and going to heaven. Some readers, who may themselves dream of becoming rich and famous, will feel that Germaine misses out. The Christian tradition that made Germaine a saint will remain confident that a great reward in heaven is the only true "happily ever after".

Abelard and the Three Gifts

Folk tales about people being given gifts are found in many cultures, and this tale has echoes of several. The structure of the story suggests that the third—and last—gift is going to be the most valuable, but interestingly it is the one which appears to have the least practical use. The tale invites readers to ponder the value of the different gifts and what they represent and to reflect on the kinds of gifts they like to receive—and to give.

The Giant by the River

This classic legend of Christopher underlies the saint's popular role as the patron saint of travellers: it provides a focus for the hope and belief that God's power and strength can protect them wherever they go.

However, the lesson for the giant by the river was rather different. His meeting with the Christ-child showed him that, as a Christian, he was called to work for good against all the forces of evil, even when they threatened to destroy him. The story of Saint Christopher is told not only as a reminder of God's protection but of the challenge to face danger in order to defeat evil.

The Golden Light

The origins of this tale must surely lie in the words of Jesus, telling his followers to let their good deeds shine in a dark world. However, it has a clear parallel with an event recounted by Mother Teresa of Calcutta. Some of her nuns visited an elderly person who was living alone, weighed down by squalid living conditions. Like the nuns in this story, they encouraged the person to clean an old lamp—the one beautiful thing they had left—and to light it when the nuns came to visit. This marked a complete transformation in the life of the old person. It stands as a heartwarming testimony to how simple deeds of kindness can bring about great changes.

The Little Juggler

Variations of this legend are told in France and Italy. They provide a cheerful reminder that living in obedience to God is in no way restricted to the more serious life of study and prayer but can include whatever talents a person delights in using.

The Good Man of Assisi

One of the tales most often told about Saint Francis of Assisi concerns the time when he preached to the birds, telling them to praise their maker. However, the early biographies of his life include many more tales of his kindness to all creatures and the way they responded to his affection. This one has particularly good story structure, with a problem at the beginning and a happy and thoroughly satisfactory ending, demonstrating how a kind deed ultimately brings a blessing to everyone.

The Fisher Princess

Unlike the poor Cinderella Saint Germaine, Elizabeth of Hungary was born with expectations of marrying a prince and living happily ever after. This story tells how that dream turned to a nightmare and how Elizabeth's faith and kindness nevertheless enabled her to be fulfilled and content.

The Three Trees

In this folk tale from America, three trees each discover something special about who Jesus is. The story provides an appealing way to link the message of the popular festivals of Christmas and Easter, and is particularly suited to reading on either occasion.

The Easter Fire

This legend of Saint Patrick does not feature in Patrick's autobiography, the *Confession*, and is thought by some to be a symbolic tale rather than a historical one. It provides a dramatic example of faith shining out unafraid in a dark world.

The Slave Girl and Her Master

The story of Bakhita belongs to the twentieth century and is a delightful example of a shining life that is entirely credible and entirely miraculous.

The Ploughman Saint

Isidore and his wife Maria live out their faith with simplicity, honesty and generosity. As the things they do so clearly make the world a little more like heaven, it is no wonder this legend tells of them being miraculously transported into God's heaven.

Poor Little Rich Girl

This is a cautionary tale about the perils of selfishness and the joy of sharing. It is also a thought-provoking story about pilgrimage, leading the reader to reflect on whether the journey's quest is accomplished more by the things that happen on the way than by reaching the supposed destination.

The River

This folk tale has clear roots in the mythology of rain and drought but is also about the tension between clinging to tradition and being willing to leave the familiar in order to find the things that truly give life.

The Monk and the Mice

Martin de Porres is clearly a monk in the style of Saint Francis, and his affection for all of God's creatures and ability to live in harmony with them is exemplary, providing a glimpse of a truly peaceable world.

The Secret Giftbringer

This legend of Saint Nicholas is understood to be the inspiration behind all the tales of Santa Claus. It underpins the Christmas spirit of love and generosity that can transform people's lives.

The Fourth Wise Man

The Bible story of wise men coming to worship the baby Jesus names three gifts but does not say how many wise men there were: it is a different tradition that links the gifts to just three wise men. As a result, many tales and legends have arisen about a possible fourth wise man and the most appropriate gift to bring the Son of God.

Grandfather's Boat

This is a tale about saying goodbye. It provides a picture of the Christian hope that death is not the end, but simply a horizon beyond which people cannot see.